Pasto
Prayer Ministry
Teams in the
Local Church

Letters to Avril

*A series of letters to a friend
who is interested in setting up a
Pastoral Prayer Ministry Team
within her church*

Ruth Hawkey

New Wine Press

New Wine Press
PO Box 17
Chichester
England PO20 6YB

Bible quotations are taken from the New King James Version, copyright
1983 by Thomas Nelson, Inc.

ISBN 1 903725 15 1

Typeset by CRB Associates, Reepham, Norfolk.
Printed in England by Clays Ltd, St Ives plc.

Acknowledgements

Joe and Ruth Hawkey would like to thank Ed and Liz Harding (New Wine Publishers) for their invaluable support and continued investment into their ministry. Also Merle Williams our editor and friend, who along with Paul her husband has given us much encouragement along the way. Thanks are also due to Ellel Ministries for the invaluable experience we gained as we worked alongside them as well as the many friends who have allowed us to share our understanding of forming Pastoral Prayer Ministry Teams within their church.

Preface

As Joe and I have travelled around the country visiting a number of fellowships and churches teaching about the work of the Holy Spirit and His wonderful gifts of healing, we often see a need for prayer ministry amongst the folk. Jesus said that He came to *'heal the brokenhearted, To preach deliverance to the captives And recovery of sight to the blind, To set at liberty those who are oppressed, To preach the acceptable year of the LORD'* (Luke 4:18–19) and whenever His people come together, He is always reaching out to heal and to set people free.

As people's needs surface this raises a number of questions within the fellowship, such as: 'How do I go about having a Pastoral Prayer Ministry Team established in my church?' Or as one Pastor said: 'Help! I cannot cope with all of my people's needs. What can I do to share the load?'

Many churches do have people available who will pray for others and who do so adequately. Sometimes, however, they feel in need of a much more structured approach, or perhaps that they need training in order that they may pray more effectively. One lady said to me recently, 'We pray for one another on an ad hoc basis and God blesses us but we feel that He is encouraging us to train a team of people who are called and equipped to pray healing into the lives of others in our fellowship. Help! How do we set about building such a team?' This book *Letters to Avril* is an answer to her cry, for it was developed in response to her and other churches' needs, and we trust that it will be helpful to many in the Body of Christ.

Ruth Hawkey

Contents

Letter 1

'What Exactly Is a Pastoral Prayer Ministry Team?'

Dear Avril,

You asked me recently if I would describe for you what I mean by a Pastoral Prayer Ministry Team and what it would actually look like. I'm afraid that I am finding that rather difficult to answer, for in every church it will probably look slightly different. Basically it is a group of people who have a deep interest in the healing ministry and who feel that the Lord is calling them to pray for the folk within their church who are in need of physical, spiritual or emotional healing. They will probably have been reading and studying the healing ministry of Jesus for quite a long while, reflecting on the Scriptures as to His method of healing as well as perusing everything that they can find on the subject. Undoubtedly they will have been listening to tapes on the topic and may have been on a number of courses about the healing ministry.

They will most likely be the kind of people to whom others are drawn when they are in trouble and probably will already be doing pastoral care in one form or another. One day, either because of some challenging teaching concerning the call of Christ to the churches to *'heal the brokenhearted'* (Isaiah 61:1; Luke 4:18) or through the influence of what is happening in other places, they begin to realise that a Pastoral Prayer Ministry Team is needed in 'their' church. They probably also realise that being part of such a team would fulfil their own calling, and so with others in the church such a team would begin to be formed. As I said earlier, the format of such a team would depend upon the needs of the church but I would recommend that you consider using the 'medical model' which Joe and I have introduced and used to good effect in a number of churches. The 'medical model' consists of people who are trained in a variety of ways in order to function as 'carers, pharmacists, doctors and consultants'. Such a team, much as it would in the medical world, will be able to meet the multitude of needs within the church. You might like also to consider using the expertise of those in the congregation who have secular jobs involving some of the counselling and educa-tional skills or knowledge that your prayer team would find helpful both as a resource or to train your team. I hope that you find this helps you Avril, and I will try to elaborate more on the format of such a team in the near future as we continue to share ideas.

Love in Jesus

Ruth

Letter 2

'Why Do We Need a Pastoral Prayer Ministry Team?'

Dear Avril,

I am so glad that you are beginning to get a vision of a group of people within your own church that will be used to bring healing to those in need. You asked me why I feel so strongly that every church should have a Pastoral Prayer Ministry Team. Well of course there are a number of reasons for this, but as I see it the main one is simply that it is an essential part of the church's job description: to preach, heal and deliver (see Luke 9:1–2). Jesus was always looking to heal the broken-hearted and the Body of Christ is called upon to continue that work until He comes again. The healing ministry is as much a part of the Church's mission as is the saving of souls and the social gospel. There are of course many other reasons such as:

- When God speaks, He is looking for an opportunity to minister to us in a deep and a meaningful way. There needs therefore to be a group of people – a 'Pastoral Prayer Ministry Team' for instance – who are available to pray with the folk whom God is touching through His Word.

- Today, perhaps more than at any other time in the Church's history, people are experimenting with drugs, the occult, sexual relationships etc. Therefore, when they become Christians they will need cleansing, healing and deliverance. As part of the evangelistic programme of a church there will need to be people who are trained and who therefore know how to pray into these areas.

- When we are in difficulties, it is often necessary and helpful if another person is present to help us to grow through our pain. Christians are not exempt from hurts and wounds. The challenge is to grow in holiness, and the Pastor is unlikely to be able to meet all of these pastoral needs on his own. Some Christians may sadly become disillusioned, doubting that Jesus really can heal their deepest grief and pain.

- The church cannot grow and prosper if a number of people within the body are wounded. It therefore makes sense to make sure that prayer and healing is available for them when they request it.

- If the church is to serve the area in which they live, they will need to make provision for those who come for help.

I hope this gives you some guidance, Avril, as you try to clarify and share your vision with others as to why a Pastoral Prayer Ministry Team is so necessary within your local fellowship.

Love in Jesus

Ruth

Letter 3

'Where Do We Begin?'

Dear Avril,

As you quite rightly say, 'It's OK having the vision for a Pastoral Prayer Ministry Team within the church and being able to see the great need for it, but where do I begin?' I'll try to answer that as best as I can, realising of course that it is always a good idea to begin with prayer! Having said that, there are a number of important steps, which you will need to take in order to make effective progress.

- It is very important that you start to pray into the vision yourself first. You need to hear the Father's heart for the broken and the wounded and align your heart with His, for it is out of the heart that the mouth speaks, and therefore you will most naturally share the vision if it is planted firmly in your own heart first. I am encouraged that you say that this is already beginning to happen.

- It is also vital that you begin to pray for another person to draw alongside you who will agree with you in prayer, for it really is a case of *'if two of you agree ... it will be done'* (Matthew 18:19). Maybe you could ask the Lord to bring another person alongside you who is already beginning to get excited about the healing ministry, and who will share with you in helping to bring a team into being.

• Next, please take time out to share your vision for a team to be established with the leadership. It is essential that they too begin to realise the necessity of having a trained group of people within the church, therefore it is worth spending as much time as possible praying that they also will see the need.

Most church leaders will recognise that some of the deeper needs of their people cannot be met through the traditionally accepted activities of church life alone. A minister, pastor or vicar cannot do everything. Leaders are responsible for the pastoral needs of their people and they are sometimes reluctant to share the job with others for a number of different reasons. Consequently, they often wear themselves out. One of the answers is for them to choose and train a team who can work with them and who are under their direction. Be patient Avril, and wait for the leadership to take the initiative. It is very important, as you probably know, never to condemn or put the leadership down in the meantime.

• The next step will be to share your vision with other people within the church whom God will lead you to. You will probably find that there are a number of people who already have a heart for the broken, for the hurt and the needy and they are simply waiting for someone to verbalise how they have been feeling. I can't remember whether you are a house group leader or a cell group leader, but either way you will most likely be taking the opportunity to pray for people in your group, and it may be possible for you to share the vision with them.

If you are a member of such a group, rather than the leader, then you could suggest to the leadership that it might be a good and helpful thing to pray regularly for one another. Be patient. God will bring it to pass if it is of Him. One lady prayed into her vision for a number of years before her church was ready to begin a Pastoral Prayer Ministry Team and it was simply through her faithfulness and perseverance that one was eventually established. Remember that Habakkuk says that the vision may be slow in coming but *'Though it tarries, wait for it; Because it will surely come'* (Habakkuk 2:3).

- Whilst you are waiting for the vision to be accepted by the church and the leadership, you will need to continue to get training for yourself, and with the leadership's approval, suggest courses etc. to others. One lady whom I met whilst in Canada, trained up a small team with her Pastor's approval (even though he didn't really see the need himself for such a team within the church). It was a very exciting day when he rang to seek her help for someone who was in desperate need and he didn't have the time or the ability to deal with her himself. 'We need a team of trained people' was his cry.

- Maybe you could suggest speakers on the subject of healing for special church events such as anniversaries etc., as well as looking for other opportunities to bring the healing ministry to the notice of others within the church and area, however please **don't become a bore**! Test your vision by mixing with others who have a similar call and read, study, mark and learn all that you can in the waiting period. Ask God to provide someone who knows more than you do, so that you can learn from them.

- Ask God to show you the people within the congregation for whom you might privately intercede, praying that He might give you the eyes to see those with hurts and pain. Then begin to pray for them with as much faith as you can muster, asking that they may be touched and healed. If your heart is to see children healed, there is a very good book on intercession by a woman called Beryl Burgess. It is called *Dear Mark & Sarah* published by New Wine Press.

- It is also very important to remember when considering the formation of a Pastoral Prayer Ministry Team, not to pray for healing with others without your leadership's consent. I would counsel you to earn your right by learning submission. In the meantime you can discover a lot about how to support and care for hurting people by lending a listening ear and showing a compassionate heart towards them.

Love in Jesus

Ruth

Letter 4

Leadership Is Vital

Dear Avril,

You are quite right when you say that you feel that it is very important to get your leadership involved if you want to have a Pastoral Prayer Ministry Team established within your fellowship. When **they** have caught the vision that you have hidden and nurtured in your heart, it will take great strides forward to fruition because there are a number of things which only leadership can do.

- For example, they are in a prime position to teach the congregation the importance of the healing ministry as part of Christ's commission to the church. If they so desire, they will have the opportunity to preach a series of sermons on the healing ministry. For example: 'How Jesus healed', 'Does God heal today?', 'Has God still got a heart for the broken?', 'Is God interested in healing relationships?' etc., so raising the topic of healing amongst the congregation. This will undoubtedly cause people to ask the very relevant question: 'That is all very well but where are the people who are going to be praying for others alongside our over-worked pastor?'

This will give leadership the chance to share the vision with the congregation as the opportunities arise.

- Leaders are in a prime position to demonstrate the power of the Holy Spirit in their own personal ministry. This will not only encourage people to seek ministry themselves, but will also raise the need for others to be trained to help the leader. I will be praying for you Avril, as you share your thoughts with your leadership.

Love in Jesus

Ruth

Letter 5

Choosing a Team

Dear Avril,

Yes of course I am very happy to suggest a course of action to help you to take your ministry team forward. I will use some of the material, which I have sent to you in my recent correspondence with the proviso that you feel free to adapt it to your own personal church situation.

As I mentioned in one of my earlier letters, it is better to begin by exploring the subject of 'healing' with the entire congregation on a Sunday, as this will help everyone in the church to feel that they are a part of what is happening. We would suggest that the minister/pastor or visiting preacher preach a number of sermons on the 'Healing Ministry'.

You would then follow up the Sunday services with a midweek meeting for those people who want to explore further as to whether they are called to be part of a healing team within the church. At this meeting you will probably find that there are a number of folk who are interested in the healing ministry but whose primary gift is as intercessors or intrepid evangelists, rather than people who are suitable to pray in a longer and deeper way into other people's lives. It is important that they also discover where their gifting fits into the life of the church.

To discover who may be on your eventual Pastoral Prayer Ministry Team I suggest that a topic, which you may care to discuss, would be: 'What kind of qualities will a Pastoral Prayer Ministry Team person possess?' You may decide to give them the following 'Attributes of a Pastoral Prayer Ministry Team Member' sheet to complete. I will put this on a separate page (see page 23), so that you can photocopy it if you feel that it would be useful.

You may also decide to give them the questionnaire 'Questions to Ask Oneself' (see page 24) to return in due time.

You would then use your own discernment, Avril, and the sheets which they have completed, to form a judgement as to who should be a part of the team and who should be the intercessors or the evangelists etc. Please don't take people on board simply out of sympathy, for your team will be dealing with very vulnerable and hurting people within the church. It is best if you have established criteria, as this will give you an objective basis on which to work. Approach with wisdom and caution the people you feel are God's provision; approach them sensitively; allow them time to pray and to seek God for themselves as to whether they should be a part of the team. Be aware that they may already be over-committed. It is sometimes quite difficult to extricate someone who proves to be unsuitable at a later stage.

If people approach you to be on the team, it is better to press the pause button and suggest a time of praying about it than to incorporate the wrong people. You will need to weigh each person carefully and the following are the sort of questions, which you should be asking:

- What is their *Christian commitment*?

  - Their ability to submit to the lordship of Christ

  - Their ability to submit to leadership of the team/ church

  - Their ability to submit to correction and discipline

  – Their love for God's word and their love for other
   people

 (You may be already aware of much of this but check it
 out!)

- What is their *church commitment*?
  - Are they faithful in attending worship?
  - Are they supportive of the leadership?
  - Do they hold any leadership positions?
  - Are they faithful in any tasks they have undertaken so
    far?

- What is their *secular job commitment*?
  - What sort of time involvement does their job require?

- What is the *impression* you receive?
  - Are they able to make themselves clearly understood
    in conversation?
  - Are they reasonably presentable?
  - Are they approachable in manner?

- What do they understand about the *vision*?
  - The vision of the church and the ministry team
  - Are they in line with the vision or do they have their
    own?
  - Do they feel a call of God on their lives for this
    ministry?

- What is their *experience* of ministering to others?
  - In house group, church or other settings

- What steps have they taken to *train* themselves so far?
  - Books, tapes, conferences, videos.

- How much *time* do they feel they could give? (This
  would depend of course on family, job and church
  commitments.)

- Are they the sort of people to *keep confidences*?

- Are they gossips and therefore natural evangelists?

- Are they *open* to ministry themselves?
  - Are they healed healers?

- What is their *heart* attitude?
  - Do they have open loving hearts?

Be aware that the enemy will try to sow people into your team who will not be suitable. They may be very good people but with weaknesses that could prove fatal to your church so **be on your guard!**

Love in Jesus

Ruth

Attributes of a Pastoral Prayer Ministry Team Member

Score yourself as follows (circle as appropriate):

rarely = 1;   sometimes = 2;   often = 3;   always = 4

- I recognise and respond to people in need.   1 2 3 4
- I have a compassionate heart.   1 2 3 4
- I live a sacrificial lifestyle.   1 2 3 4
- I have the ability to empathise.   1 2 3 4
- I enjoy listening to others.   1 2 3 4
- I can discern and address the real problem.   1 2 3 4
- I don't talk too much.   1 2 3 4
- I believe the person's story.   1 2 3 4
- I allow the person to be real.   1 2 3 4
- I am willing to see the person through.   1 2 3 4
- I am fair in my dealings with people.   1 2 3 4
- I am well read in the healing ministry.   1 2 3 4
- I can keep confidences.   1 2 3 4
- I am not easily shocked.   1 2 3 4
- I am patient.   1 2 3 4
- I am unbiased.   1 2 3 4
- I am not condemnatory.   1 2 3 4
- I am not abusive in my language.   1 2 3 4
- I have a heart for the Body of Christ.   1 2 3 4
- I respect leadership.   1 2 3 4

Add up and place your marks next to the total.
You should aim for 50%!

Total marks _____

Questions to ask oneself

Ask a friend to help you, and try to be honest! Give yourself a score based on 1 to 5. Circle the one most appropriate (1 is low; 5 is high).

- Do I recognise that there are people in my church with needs? 1 2 3 4 5

- How compassionate is my heart for the hurting? 1 2 3 4 5

- How prepared am I to put others needs before my own? 1 2 3 4 5

- How good am I at being kind to people? 1 2 3 4 5

- Am I able to identify and have empathy with someone in need? 1 2 3 4 5

- How good am I at reading clues from people's language/behaviour? 1 2 3 4 5

- Am I a good listener? 1 2 3 4 5

- How well read am I in the healing ministry? 1 2 3 4 5

- Am I tactful? 1 2 3 4 5

- Do I find it hard to be judgmental about others? 1 2 3 4 5

- Am I patient? 1 2 3 4 5

- Am I unbiased in my opinions about people? 1 2 3 4 5

- Do I have a heart to pray for the needy people in my church? 1 2 3 4 5

- Am I able to keep confidences? 1 2 3 4 5

- Do I believe people when they are sharing their story with me? 1 2 3 4 5

- Do I respect others and their views? 1 2 3 4 5

Total your score. Aim for 50% marks!

Total marks _____

Letter 6

'What Does My Team Need to Know?'

Dear Avril,

Help! I'm not sure that I know where to start in order to answer the question: 'What does my Pastoral Prayer Ministry Team need to know?' Perhaps the best place would be to assure you that we ourselves cannot know everything and that even if we did we could not bring about anyone's healing. That is the work of the Holy Spirit alone. We are simply called upon to be available to listen to the person share their story and then call upon Him for His gifts. These will include discernment, wisdom, and gifts of healing and even sometimes of miracles! It is also important to remember that when praying for someone there is 'no technique'! We have to come fresh each time to the Holy Spirit and learn how to rely upon Him. Therefore, it is relevant that the Pastoral Prayer Ministry Team is familiar with the following areas:

- The gifts of the Holy Spirit and how to use them.

- How to be soaked in and apply the Word of God, which is the Sword of the Spirit, to their own lives as well as into the lives of others.

- Depending on the format and the requirements of the ministry team, they may also need to know how to minister into various situations. For example:
  - The causes of **emotional damage**, and how various people respond to it.
  - The deep hold **rejection** can have on a person's life.
  - The devastation which can take place if someone has been **sexually abused**.
  - The place of the **deliverance** ministry: when it is necessary and when it is not.
  - The place for **spiritual warfare** and how to intercede for ourselves, our families and for others in this area.
- Then there are the specialist subject areas such as the occult, marital breakdown, bereavement and freemasonry to name but a few, which certainly the consultants on your team will need to know.

I would advise you Avril, to hold a series of training seminars, either led by yourself if you feel able, or with qualified people to visit you to do some teaching. Our suggested programme of basic training, for all levels of Pastoral Prayer Ministry Team (if only for insight into the hurts and wounds, which people may have suffered), would be the following:

- The **healing ministry of Jesus**, His principles and practices.

- How **man is made** and the various parts of his being where he can be sick (i.e. physically, his emotional area, mentally or in his spirit).

- They will, as we have already noted, need to know how to **discern** the gifts of the Holy Spirit and how to **listen to Him** and to the person in need of help, at the same time!

There are also some very important basic keys to healing, which are vital for the ministry team to be aware of when they are praying for others. One would be the importance of forgiveness and how we can be bonded in both a good and a bad way to people around us. They will also need to learn 'how to' pray into different areas of pain. You will also be required to teach into many other areas, such as the place of curses, generational sin, abuse, inner vows as well as pronouncements. Remember that training and equipping will need to be an ongoing process and that this training is best left 'open' for anyone, who is interested, so that you do not create a 'superior group'. Keep going Avril you're doing a great job!

Love in Jesus

Ruth

Letter 7

A Basic Training Manual

Dear Avril,

I'm so glad that you found my previous letter helpful but I quite understand that you feel that you need a more detailed training scheme for your team. Please forgive my delay in getting back to you, but here, at last, is the outline of training, which I promised you a few weeks ago. I envisage that you will meet with your team one evening a week for approximately eight to ten weeks and that each session will last approximately two hours, for example 7.30 until 9.30. I suggest Avril that the evening sessions follow the same format:

Format
Worship (20 minutes)
Teaching (30 minutes)
Individual activity (20 minutes)
Group activity/Prayers (30 minutes)
Debriefing/Final prayer (20 minutes)

I will suggest the topic which should be taught at each session and give you a brief outline as to how we would approach it with one or two ideas to start you thinking. It is important that the topics are scriptural as well as being practically based, with plenty of illustrations. These **teachings** will give your team some insight into the situations with which they may be confronted within the church. I assume that you will put your own thoughts and scriptures into place.

I will also give you some suggestions as to what the **individual activity** would be for each evening session and envision that this would take approximately twenty minutes. It sometimes helps to serve a cup of coffee at this time as well! The individual work would be followed by a **group activity** which could be used in a number of ways i.e. praying for one another for expressed needs, studying some relevant scriptures together or discussing the teaching. I will give you some suggestions but am very happy for you to adapt them to your own particular church.

I have put each session on a new page (for ease of reference – see pages 30–53) and it will be helpful if all of the members of the team have a copy of the training sessions so that they can work through them together. I hope that these will help you Avril to do more training with your burgeoning team!

Love in Jesus

Ruth

SESSION 1

Teaching: 'God's heart for healing'

> *'If you diligently heed the voice of the LORD your God and do what is right in His sight, give ear to His commandments and keep all His statutes, I will put none of the diseases on you which I have brought on the Egyptians. For I am the LORD who heals you.'*   (Exodus 15:26)

Points

- Search the Scriptures noting that God has a heart to bring healing and health to His people.

- Note that Jesus' heart was also to heal, using scriptural references to back up the teaching.

- One of the gifts of the Holy Spirit is that of 'healings'. Therefore, God the Father, God the Son and God the Holy Spirit has a desire to heal in the church today.

Resource material

The Scriptures.
Healing from the Inside Out, Tom Marshall, Sovereign World.
The Power to Heal, Francis MacNutt, Hodder and Stoughton.

Individual activity

Taking a spiritual history

- Take a sheet of paper and about halfway down the page draw a line from left to right. At the far right pencil in the current year and at the far left write the year you were born.

- Insert along the top of the timeline when you were converted, and any events of significance in your personal spiritual history.

- On the back of your sheet, write three influential books, which you have read, excluding the Bible.
- Write down the names of three influential people in your spiritual history.

Group activity/prayers

- Share your thoughts with others in the group as to how God has led you.
- Share about the time you committed your life to God.
- Describe the books to the members of the group and say why they have affected you.
- Choose one of the influential people and share with the group as to why they are important to you.
- Pray for one another in the group.

Project to be completed at home and returned the following week

- Go through the Gospels with three coloured pens.
- Mark all **physical** healing with first colour, e.g. blue.
- Mark all **inner healing** with the second colour, e.g. green.
- Mark all **deliverance** healing with third colour, e.g. red.

SESSION 2

Teaching: 'The healing ministry of Jesus'

> 'The Spirit of the LORD is upon Me,
> Because He has anointed Me to preach the gospel
>   to the poor;
> He has sent Me to heal the brokenhearted,
> To preach deliverance to the captives
> And recovery of sight to the blind,
> To set at liberty those who are oppressed.'

(Luke 4:18)

Points

- Principles and practices of Jesus:
  - How Jesus chose His team – after much prayer.
  - How He equipped His team – on the job training.
  - How He sent His team out – in two's.

- How man is made: spirit, body and soul (mind, emotions and will).

- How we can be ill in any of these areas and therefore in need of healing.

Resource material

The Scriptures.
Power Healing, John Wimber, Hodder and Stoughton.

Individual activity

Complete the following Ministry Team Questionnaire.

Name: .... **Telephone no:** ....

- Do you feel the call of God to be part of the Pastoral Prayer Ministry Team within the church?

....

- Write briefly, about how long you have been a Christian and when it happened.

  ....

  ....

- Do you feel able to commit yourself to the church and come under the discipline of its leadership in ministry team training and practice?

  ....

- What reasons do you have for wanting to be a part of the Ministry Team?

  ....

  ....

- What is your experience of ministering to others, so far? (Don't worry if you are a complete novice.)
  - ☐ Many times in public   ☐ Often in private
  - ☐ Occasionally in private   ☐ Novice
  - ☐ Few times in public

- What time would you be able to offer? Consider your commitments to family, work and other church roles. For example:

Occasional Sundays after service	Yes	No
Occasional mid-week sessions	Yes	No
Ongoing training commitment	Yes	No

- What steps have you taken to learn more about the Healing Ministry? For example, what and how many books have you read?

  ....

  ....

- What previous courses and seminars have you attended?

  ....

  ....

- Can you treat everyone equally and confidentially?

....

- Are you open to have ministry yourself, if the Lord shows you an area of need?

....

- What other areas of training would you like to have in the healing ministry? Please list the topics which you would like to see covered in future training courses.

....

Group activity/prayers

The leader invites anyone that wishes to have prayer to sit on a centrally placed chair, around which the rest of the group gathers. Making **use of oil** spend some time praying for healing for those who request it (James 5:13–18). Encourage the use of the gifts of the Holy Spirit.

- The person is asked the question: 'Why have you requested prayer?'
- The group prays for them and anoints them with oil, making the sign of the cross in the Name of Jesus.
- The leader would then enquire as to whether anyone has a word of knowledge or a scripture etc. for the person.
- Continue until all of those requiring prayer have been prayed for.

Project to be completed at home and returned the following week

- Search the Scriptures to find out what methods Jesus used in order to bring people to a place of healing? For example, if and when He used the laying on of hands; when He used touch; was faith needed?; etc.
- Make a list of His methods and share them with the team next week.

SESSION 3

Teaching: 'The Holy Spirit and His gifts'

(1 Corinthians 12:4–10)

Points

- Who is the Holy Spirit?
- What does He bring to the Christian?
- Give instances of Jesus using the gifts of the Holy Spirit.
- How are His gifts to be used in the healing ministry today?

Resource material

The Scriptures.
There are many good books concerning the work of the Holy Spirit and His gifts.
Know Your Spiritual Gifts, Mark Stibbe, Marshall Pickering.

Individual activity

Do a timeline chart regarding the work of the Holy Spirit within your own life.

- Take a sheet of paper and about halfway down the page draw a line from left to right. At the far right, pencil in the current year. At the far left, write the year you were born.
- Mark on the timeline the occasions when another person has ministered healing, a prophecy, or a word of knowledge to you through the Holy Spirit.
- Mark on the timeline the occasions when you have been used by the Holy Spirit to speak a word of healing or encouragement into another person's life.

Group activity/prayers

We suggest that you begin this session with a declaration of the lordship of Jesus

Prayer

Thank you Jesus for dying on the Cross to set me free
from my sin. I now choose to declare that you are Lord of
every area of my life. Lord of my home and my family.
Lord of my time and my possessions. Lord of my work
and my finances. Lord of my thoughts and my emotions.
Lord of my decisions and my future and Lord of my
ministry. Please fill me afresh with your Holy Spirit. I give
myself, spirit, soul and body to you. Thank you for being
my Lord. Amen.

Ways of developing the gifts of the Holy Spirit:

- Put your team into groups of four to six people and ask
  them to share together which **gifts of the Holy Spirit** they
  have used in the past.

- If the people are well known to each other, they can share
  what they believe are the gifts of the other people in the
  group.

- The people in the group then share **their desire** to be
  used by the Holy Spirit in other gifts and the person on
  their left prays for them to receive the gift.

- The leader **encourages** each person to put in a scripture, a
  word of knowledge, a word of wisdom, and speaking in
  tongues, as they feel led by the Holy Spirit.

- The group then **waits on the Lord for Him to speak**.
  Encourage the people not to be afraid of silence and to
  have the faith to step out and take a risk if they feel God is
  giving them a word for the group.

- Ask the group the following questions: 'Does anyone in
  the group respond to a word, or a scripture, which has
  been given?' 'Does anyone in the group have a person or
  a family member to whom it could apply?'

- Encourage the group to share in which way they feel they
  could be more open to the Holy Spirit.

- If it seems right, the group members could pray for one person within the group who has a particular need, asking the Holy Spirit to minister through them.

Project to be completed at home and returned the following week

- Read: Acts 2:38; Romans 12:6–8; 1 Corinthians 12:4–11, 28; Ephesians 4:11.
- Do you have one of these gifts?
- Who in your church has one of these gifts?
- Do you know another Christian with a specific gift? Consider how they use it?
- Read Romans 12:9–18 and Galatians 5:22–23.
- What evidence is there that the fruit of the Spirit is growing in your life?
- What evidence is there of the fruit of the Spirit in the life of your church?
- Write down what gifts and fruit you would like God to develop over the next ten months in your life. Be willing to share your hopes with another member of the Pastoral Prayer Ministry Team.

SESSION 4

Teaching: 'Learning to listen'

> *'Jesus said to her, "Go, call your husband, and come here."'*
> (John 4:16)

Points

- The importance of listening to God.

- The importance of listening to the person.

- Learning to listen with all of your senses (noting the person's body language, if there is any tension etc.).

- The necessity of asking relevant questions: e.g. 'Why have you asked for prayer?' 'When did the problem begin?' 'Are there any other members of your family with a similar problem?' etc.

Resource material

The Scriptures
Some of the 'Samaritan' material is very good in this area of listening.
Swift to Hear, Michael Jacobs, S.P.C.K.
Teach Yourself Body Language, Gordon R. Wainwright, Teach Yourself Books.

Individual activity

Select one of the following two statements and respond to it:

- 'The reason I have been involved in the healing ministry'

- 'The reason I have not, until now, been involved in the healing ministry'

Group activity/prayers

Please choose one of the following activities.

Listening and taking notes

Divide your team into groups of three.

The first person **narrates** a story to the other two in the group, concerning something that happened to them the day before. The second person **listens** and asks open-ended questions, whilst the third person takes **notes**. They then discuss together what has been shared and pray for any expressed needs. They then change places until all have told a story, listened or have taken notes.

Observation of body language

Divide your team into groups of three.

Give one person a pre-planned story to **share** with the other two. The second individual **listens** and draws out the narrative whilst the third person **observes** the one who is listening, noting their attitude, body language and the type of questions asked. The observer then shares his findings with the other two. Each person takes it in turn to become the storyteller, the listener and the observer.

For the above activities chose from the following stories.

▶ Story 1

Person: A woman married with two children, one of whom is slightly deaf.
Background: She is one of three children. Her parents were divorced when she was ten years old. They have moved around the country many times because her father was in the army.
Presenting problem: Prayer for migraine headaches.
Underlying problem: Panic attacks, which appear unexpectedly.

▶ Story 2

Person: A single person. Career orientated with elderly parents.
Background: She is an only child, her father is a solicitor, and her mother is a teacher. They are both Christians.

Presenting problem: Prayer for better sleeping patterns.
Underlying problem: Very lonely and depressed. Has a desire to be married.

▶ Story 3

Person: An elderly person whose partner has recently died.
Background: He was single for many years and looked after his parents until they died. He never grieved for them and filled the pain of the loss by getting married shortly afterwards.
Presenting problem: Prayer for various aches and pains (arthritis).
Underlying problem: He feels very lonely and grief stricken and is contemplating remarriage.

Project to be completed at home and returned the following week

- List some of the reasons as to why the Christian healing ministry should be brought back into the life of the church.

- List three reasons why we should have public healing services.

- How do you think the healing ministry could be integrated into your church?

- Draw up a brief plan to share with the other members of the team next week.

SESSION 5

Teaching: 'The importance of forgiveness'

'Take heed to yourselves. If your brother sins against you, rebuke him; and if he repents, forgive him. And if he sins against you seven times in a day, and seven times in a day returns to you, saying, "I repent," you shall forgive him.'
(Luke 17:3–4)

Points
- God's forgiveness of my sin.
- My need to forgive others.
- My need to forgive myself.
- Forgiveness is a choice.

Resource material

The Scriptures.
Forgiveness, Kevin Smith, Sovereign World.

Individual activity

- Allow ten to fifteen minutes to make a 'forgiveness' list of people who may have caused offence: mum, dad, spouse, friends, church, work place, God, self, and any others.
- Choose to forgive each person on the list.
- Asterisk the ones that will need to be dealt with later.
- Answer the following questions:
  What good things did they put into my life?
  ....
  ....
  What things do I have to thank them for?
  ....
  ....

What bad things have they put into my life?

....

....

What do I need to forgive them for?

....

....

Group activity/prayers

- Divide into groups of four to six people, give each person one of the following scriptures: Matthew 5:7; Matthew 6:14–15; Matthew 18:21–22; Mark 11:24–25; Luke 6:36; Luke 17:3–4.

- Ask them to take a few moments silently reading and praying into the scriptures concerning forgiveness and then share their findings with the rest of the group.

- Divide the group into pairs to share with each other their forgiveness list, talking through any particularly difficult issues.

- Ask the person to speak out the names of the people they are choosing to forgive.

Use the following prayers of forgiveness and repentance.

A prayer of repentance for their own personal sin

Heavenly Father I thank you for the forgiveness, which you offer me, through the death of Jesus Christ upon the Cross. I agree with your verdict on my sin, that the punishment is death. Thank you that Jesus died in my place. I freely and gladly confess my sin [*ask the person to speak out anything specific*] and I turn away from it in the name of Jesus. I choose to turn from my sinful ways and go your way from this day and I thank you, in Jesus' name. Amen.

A prayer of forgiveness

> Heavenly Father, I thank you that Jesus died upon the cross to take away my sins. Thank you that you have forgiven me. I now choose, by an act of my will, to stand with your command to forgive those who have hurt me. I therefore freely forgive [*name of person*] for all of the harm and the hurt, which he/she has caused me. I freely release him/her into the freedom of my forgiveness. I ask you to release me now from all of the consequences of the hurt and pain in Jesus' name. Amen.

Project to be completed at home and returned the following week

- Consider the following stories in Scripture. Where and from whom would forgiveness be needed?
  - Peter and his denial of Jesus (Mark 14:66–72).
  - Naomi and the death of her husband and sons (Ruth 1:1–5).
  - Hannah and her longing for children (1 Samuel 1:1–18)
- Make a forgiveness list for Peter, Naomi and Hannah.
- Are there any other people in their stories who may need to forgive them?
- Make a forgiveness list for these people too.
- Draw up a format of ministry for Peter, Naomi and Hannah, looking especially at the way you would lead them to a place of forgiveness.

SESSION 6

Teaching: 'Relationships'

David and Jonathan

> *'And it was so, when he had finished speaking to Saul, the soul of Jonathan was knit to the soul of David, and Jonathan loved him as his own soul.'*   (1 Samuel 18:1)

Points

- Explain the concept of 'bonding' looking at the following scriptures: Genesis 44:30 (parent); Matthew 19:5 (spouse); 1 Samuel 18:1 (friendship).

- How do we form emotional bonding with people: a parent, spouse, family, and friends?

- Some bondings are good and some bondings are bad:

  > *'If your brother, the son of your mother, your son or your daughter, the wife of your bosom, or your friend who is as your own soul, secretly entices you . . . '*
  >
  >   (Deuteronomy 13:6–7)

- How can we be set free?

Resource material

The Scriptures.
Right Relationships, Tom Marshall, Sovereign World.
Feed My Sheep, Feed My Lambs, Harold Dewberry, New Wine Press (out of print).

Individual activity

- Make a list of your relationships with the following people: mother, father, siblings, spouse (if applicable), children (if applicable), friends, work colleagues, church friends.

- Note the good and bad emotions, which they have inputted into your life.

Group activity/prayers

- Divide the group into pairs to talk through their lists.
- Pray through the list with their partner. The following is a pattern which you may use:

  (a) The person first repents of his or her own sin and their partner speaks out forgiveness (see the forgiveness prayer in Session 3).

  (b) The person then chooses to forgive the one who has wronged them.

  (c) The partner cuts the ungodly bond between the person and the one who has wronged them, using oil if preferred. Speak out the Word of God: *'If the Son makes you free, you shall be free indeed'* (John 8:36).

  (d) The partner then lifts off anything that may have come to the person through the ungodly bonding.

  (e) The partner then speaks into the person the opposite of whatever negatives they discern have been placed on the person. For example if there has been manipulation and control, then lift that off and speak in freedom. Break each bonding separately and systematically.

  (f) Use the following prayer.

Prayer

In the name of Jesus Christ of Nazareth, I break every ungodly spirit, soul or body bonding between [*name*] and [*name*]. I take the sword of the Spirit, which is the Word of God, and I declare that [*name*] is set free from any hold, either natural or demonic which [*name*] has had over her/him. I place the Cross of Jesus Christ between [*name*] and [*name*] and declare that all ungodliness be drawn to the Cross. Amen.

Project to be completed at home and returned the following week

- Consider Jacob and his family. List the possible good and bad bondings.

SESSION 7

Teaching: 'Dealing with emotional pain'

Peter and his betrayal of Jesus

> 'And a second time the rooster crowed. And Peter called to
> mind the word that Jesus had said to him, "Before the
> rooster crows twice, you will deny Me three times." And
> when he thought about it, he wept.' (Mark 14:72)

Points

- Causes of emotional pain: parents, trauma, etc.
- The hold of rejection.
- Ways of dealing with pain.
- Praying for inner healing.

Resource material

The Scriptures.
Deep Wounds, Deep Healing, Charles H. Kraft, Servant
    Publications.
Healing of Damaged Emotions, D. Seamands, Scripture Press.
Healing Emotional Wounds, Ruth Hawkey, New Wine Press.

Individual activity

Consider the following questions:

- Were you allowed to express emotions in your family?

  ....

- Have you ever felt rejected?

  ....

- Have you ever suffered a trauma in the past?

  ....

- What are some of the emotions which you would find difficult to express?

....

....

....

Group activity/prayers

- Divide into groups of three, spend some time discussing the above questions.
- Consider why it is sometimes difficult to share our emotions with other people.
- What strategies do we use to avoid pain?
- Pray for one another for any healing that may be needed.

Project to be completed at home and returned the following week

- Consider one situation in your life, which you found painful or difficult.
- Ask yourself the following questions:

  Where was I suffering: in my spirit, soul or in my body?

  Was God present?

  ....

  How did He show Himself?

  ....

  Has the situation been dealt with?

  ....

  Am I open to others praying with me in these situations?

  ....

  How vulnerable am I willing to be?

  ....

SESSION 8

Teaching: 'The power of family sin'

> '*I, the* LORD *your God, am a jealous God, visiting the iniquity of the fathers on the children to the third and fourth generations of those who hate Me.*' (Exodus 20:5)

Points

- Scriptural references to family sin.
- The importance of sowing and reaping.
- How do we deal with family sin?

Resource material

The Scriptures
Freedom from Generational Sin, Ruth Hawkey, New Wine Press.
Receiving the Gifts of the Holy Spirit, Bill Subritzky, Sovereign
  World.

Individual activity

Draw up a family tree noting any patterns travelling down the family line; e.g. depression, grief, anger, infirmity, abuse, alcoholism.

Group activity/prayers

- Discuss in pairs some of the patterns on the family tree.
- Ask the question as to whether they are present in us.
- Pray for each other using the following prayer.

A prayer confessing the sins of the family line and breaking any ungodly links

> Father I thank you that on the Cross you have dealt with my sin through the death and resurrection of the Lord Jesus Christ. I thank you too, that according to your word,

I can come and confess the sins of my ancestors. I do gladly and humbly repent of the sins, which members of my family line have committed. I especially repent of [*ask the person to speak out any specific sins which they know the family have committed*] and also any false worship in which they have been involved [*ask them to speak out any that are relevant, e.g. freemasonry, spiritualism, Buddhism, etc.*]. I ask you to forgive the sin and that you will set me free from its consequences, in Jesus name. Amen.

Project to be completed at home and returned the following week

Look at the following occult checklist and consider any family involvement:

Astrology, clairvoyance, coven involvement, crystal gazing, divining, Dungeons and Dragons, fortune-telling, gypsy curses, homeopathy, horoscopes, hypnosis, martial arts, mascots, mediums, ouija board, palmistry, pendulum diagnosis, satanism, séances, self-hypnosis, star signs, superstitions, tarot cards, transcendental meditation, ungodly therapies, witchcraft and yoga.

SESSION 9

Teaching: 'The power of words'

> 'Death and life are in the power of the tongue.'
>
> (Proverbs 18:21)

Points

- The power of positive words.
- The power of negative words.
- Influential people: parents, teachers, peer group etc.
- The power of inner vows.

Resource material

The Scriptures.
Blessings or Curse: You Can Choose, Derek Prince, Derek Prince Ministries.

Individual activity

List any positive or negative words, which have been spoken over you.

Positive	Negative
....	....
....	....
....	....
....	....

Group activity/prayers

- Divide into pairs sharing any thoughts concerning the words on the list.
- Pray for one another lifting off any negative words using the following prayer.

Prayer

> Father, I thank you that on the Cross Jesus carried my curse. I stand now in His name against any words or curses, which have been spoken against me. I believe that Satan and all of his works are under the feet of Jesus and I reject such words and curse and declare myself free in Jesus' name. Amen.

Project to be completed at home and returned the following week

- Study the following scriptures: Matthew 8:1–4, 14–15; 9:18–26; 19:13–15; Mark 1:28–31, 40–45; 5:21–43; 6:1–6; 7:32–37; 8:22–25; 9:14–29; 10:13–16; Luke 4:38–44; 5:12–16; 8:49–56; 13:11–17.

- What do these biblical texts inform us about Jesus' practice of using hands in the healing process?

SESSION 10

Teaching: 'Defeating the enemy'

> *'So the great dragon was cast out, that serpent of old, called the Devil and Satan, who deceives the whole world; he was cast to the earth, and his angels were cast out with him.'*
>
> (Revelation 12:9)

Points

- The place of Satan in the Scriptures.
- How Jesus dealt with Satan.
- How to recognise the enemy's footprints in the Christian's life: the person's story; family history; the person's behaviour and discernment.
- Praying for deliverance.

Resource material

The Scriptures.
Healing Through Deliverance (Part 1 & 2), Peter Horrobin, Sovereign World.
Deliverance and Inner Healing, John & Mark Sandford, Fleming H. Revell (a division of Baker Book House Company).
Demons Defeated, Bill Subritzky, Sovereign World.

Individual activity

- Take a few moments to consider whether you have been into any occult activity: tarot cards, ouija board, horoscopes, spiritualism, etc.
- Make a list and determine to see the co-ordinator for prayer into these areas.

Group activity/prayers

- Reflect on the following scriptures and discuss which would be the most effective in praying for someone for deliverance:
  - Consecrated oil (Mark 6:13; James 5:14)
  - The sacraments (1 Corinthians 11:23–32)
  - Laying on of hands (Luke 4:40)
- If it is appropriate the co-ordinator could pray for one person for deliverance, whilst the team observe and learn.

Project to be completed at home and returned the following week

Consider the prayer weapons provided in Scripture. Study the Bible references and meditate on how and when you may use these weapons in prayer ministry, especially deliverance.

- The name of Jesus (Mark 16:17; Acts 3:16; Philippians 2:10).
- The Holy Spirit and His gifts (Matthew 12:28; Acts 1:8; 1 Corinthians 12:4–11).
- The Word of God (Ephesians 6:17; Hebrews 4:12–13).
- The angels (Hebrews 1:13–14).
- Tongues (Acts 2:1–11).
- The blood of Jesus (Revelation 12:10–11).
- Praise and worship (Acts 16:25–26).

Letter 8

Group Activities

Dear Avril,

Hello, it's me again! How are you? I am responding to your urgent telephone call from last week, concerning your need for more group activities for your team. You say that you have a feeling that they need to develop skills in sharing together and praying for one another in small groups. As we have previously suggested the size of the group should be no more than four to six members so that everyone has the opportunity of being involved.

The following are some of the exercises, which Joe and I have used, and which seemed to have helped other teams to grow in confidence. I have again listed them for you for easy reference.

Group work

1. Consider the question: 'Do you want to be healed?'

- Study the passage John 5:1–18.

- What hindrances might Jesus have in mind that needed to be overcome when He asked: *'Do you want to be healed?'*

- Discuss in the group possible reasons for people failing to be healed.

- Pray for any known needs.

2. Discuss the apparent failure to bring healing

- Divide into groups of four to six.

- Ask whether anyone has had an experience of praying for one kind of healing but receiving another?

- Think of three people who have known apparent failure in their desire for healing.

- Write down their names and lift them to the Lord.

- The groups then write down three of their own personal needs.

- Consider any hindrances to having them answered and write them down.

- Lift your needs to the Lord.

- Agree with another person in the group to lift the needs to the Lord on a regular basis during the week, and report to the group at the next meeting any healing which they are able to report.

3. Encouraging and praying for one another

- Put your team into groups of around six people. Each person is asked the question, 'How are you?' After each one has answered honestly, the group speaks out words of encouragement to one another. The group then divides into pairs and the person on the right gives a word of encouragement to the person on their left and prays for them.

- The people in the group are then asked the question: 'What do you want God to do for you today?' After each one has answered honestly they again divide into pairs and this time the person on the left listens to and prays for the person on their right, asking that God will give them the desire of their heart.

4. Role-play

- The Pastoral Prayer Ministry Team co-ordinator, or an experienced person, works with a volunteer from the group. They talk together sharing an invented story or an expressed need (if the person feels able) in order to highlight how to progress with ministry.

- The group members **listen** and observe, making notes of important points. Later there needs to be a time of sharing and questioning as to why certain things happened and how the ministry would progress.

5. Facing disturbing stories

- Divide into groups of six.

- The leader puts in a graphic and somewhat disturbing case study.

- Everyone shares how he or she truly feels about the story.

- Each person helps another to express his or her negative feelings.

- Suggest ways to help each other to remain unshakeable (hearing stories often, reading many books etc.)

6. Case studies

▶ **Exercise A**

One large group to gather around the Pastoral Prayer Ministry Team leader who will be the person to do a demonstration model.

- Choose one person to be the person in need of help.

- The co-ordinator interviews the person and asks them about their story, which may be true or make-believe.

- The others in the group listen and note the main prayer points.

▶ **Exercise B**

Divide into groups of four to six people.

- The leader is given an anonymous case study to discuss.

- The groups share and discuss possible areas of healing which may be necessary for the person concerned.

▶ **Exercise C**

Divide into groups of three people.

- Give a case study to each group.

- One of them to act out the role.

- One person takes notes.

- One person interviews the 'one in need of help'.

- The three then share and reflect on feelings, attitudes, difficulties etc.

- They then change roles and proceed with a different case study.

▶ **Exercise D**

Divide into groups of four to six people.

- One person volunteers for ministry.

- Two people are responsible for questioning, sharing and discerning the ministry needs of the volunteer whilst the others gather around and contribute, as they feel able.

Let me know how you get on with the above activities.

Love in Jesus

Ruth

Letter 9

Practical Issues

Dear Avril,

How lovely to hear from you again and to hear how your Pastoral Prayer Ministry Team is progressing. You were asking me what would be the best way to organise your team, in order to use them most effectively during the Sunday morning services. I suppose that there is no 'best' way for it all depends upon a number of factors, for example the number of people in your team and how available they are each week. It may be that you will need to try a number of formats to see which way works best for you. If you have a large group it may be possible to have a rota of two teams, thus every second Sunday one of the teams would be on duty, or would be responsible for their own replacement.

Ideally, members of the Pastoral Prayer Ministry Team who are on duty should meet for prayer before their Sunday session, for we have found that private preparation is essential and the Lord may give words of knowledge in advance. The following are some important guidelines, which I would suggest you issue to your team:

- Usually pray man with man and woman with woman. Even better if your team is big enough work in pairs, male and female working together if possible.

- Keep focused on the person for whom you are praying. In other words keep your physical and your spiritual eyes open!

- Be prepared to ask for help from the leadership, before you get too far out of your depth.

- Ask the person any relevant questions, e.g. 'Why have you come forward for prayer?' 'When did the problem begin?' 'What do you want the Lord to do for you?'

- Pray into specific areas under the direction of the Holy Spirit, and be open to the gifts of the Spirit.

- Remember that 'pharmacy praying' is not a time for deep ministry.

- Be willing to take the person to one side if privacy is needed.

- Spend as much time as necessary with the person, but be aware of other people who may be in need of prayer.

- Don't be frightened of suggesting a private prayer session, if the needs seem to be too deep. See your Pastoral Prayer Ministry Team Co-ordinator in order to arrange an appointment.

- Be very sensitive about touching the person for whom you are praying without asking their permission first, this is especially true of men praying for women. Ask the person to put their hand on the problem area first and lay your hand on top if there is any doubt! Don't automatically assume that everyone is a 'Hugger'!

- Be aware of personal hygiene! BO and bad breath can be a real downer! It is also important to be aware of your demeanour. Women especially need to be aware of their dress!

- Be sensitive to the leader of the meeting. If they want to bring the service to a close be prepared to take your person to one side so that the congregation and the leadership are not distracted.

- Keep aware of the Pastoral Prayer Ministry Team Co-ordinator in case they want to direct you to someone who needs to be prayed for.

- If you are not on duty, please be willing to help if the Pastoral Prayer Ministry Team Co-ordinator calls you forward in an emergency.

- Don't be frightened of escorting the person back to their seat, if they are still a little distressed. You may want to suggest to them that they sit at the front of the church until the end of the service, and if so please stay with them.

- Remember that confidentiality is vital.

I hope that this will be a help to you and your team.

Love in Jesus

Ruth

Letter 10

Models of
Pastoral Prayer Ministry

Dear Avril,

I am so glad that you have taken the time to look around the various churches in your area and that you have seen that there are a number of different models of prayer ministry, which are already functioning within the different fellowships. As you so correctly say, some are helpful and some are not so beneficial and are even potentially dangerous. For example, you are right to express dismay that some churches seem to have 'one person prayer teams'!

It is usually the poor pastor or the person with pastoral oversight who sometimes has to pray alone for anyone requesting ministry! This can be very risky, in that the person who is being prayed for may transfer all of their needs onto that one person. Conversely, they may accuse the person who is doing the praying of abusing, misleading or hurting them. We would strongly advocate only praying for someone with another person alongside, except in an open church meeting. There are many reasons for this twofold ministry, the main one is that Jesus advocated it. The Scriptures assert that there is 'power in agreement' and it gives both the people praying and the one being prayed for a sense of protection. One has only to study the story of Joseph and Potiphar's wife in Genesis 39 and the accusations which she made against this godly man to realise the risks involved of **'going solo'**!

Praying alongside someone else also has great benefits in that it helps to boost confidence as you give one another much needed encouragement. Having another person present also helps to test discernment and provides a 'check' if you get it wrong. It is also helpful to have someone alongside to 'take the weight' now and again, for as you know Avril, ministry can be very draining. Praying alongside someone else is also a means of continual training, as you share experiences and knowledge with another Pastoral Prayer Ministry Team member.

Elders/house group model

This is when the elders and the house group leaders pray for folks in their groups as and when it is needed. This is a very beneficial method because the folks normally grow in trust with one another within the group, and therefore feel able to share deeper needs for prayer. Some training as to how to deal with deeper 'healing needs' would not come amiss and would help the 'helpers' grow in confidence. The next model is very similar to the elders/house group model.

Pastoral team model

This is a model that we have used quite effectively in churches where they already have a pastoral team in place. It requires you to train up the people with pastoral oversight in a number of areas within the healing ministry, so that they can pray more effectively for the people under their supervision. The pastoral team would have responsibility for a small group of people within the church. This has the advantage of them getting to know individuals more intimately, and therefore they will be able to pray more effectively into deeper issues when they arise. When they feel 'out of their depth' they would pass on to the elders or to the pastor those that are struggling with deeper or longer-term needs.

Group ministry model

This entails about five or six people meeting regularly for prayer in order to minister into each other's lives. It is usually not very long before others in the church begin to hear about this group and how the Lord is bringing His healing amongst them. They then begin to ask for ministry for themselves or for their friends and they are then prayed for one by one until many in the church and in the neighbourhood experience healing.

Medical model

This is a model that Joe and I have developed ourselves and which we have found most helpful within the church setting as most people can understand the concept involved. Ideally, every Pastoral Prayer Ministry Team will have a mixture of the following people on their team:

- To begin with, there will be the **carers**. These are the kind of folk who have a real gift for drawing alongside and empathising with other people. One woman, who was a friend of mine, was excellent at being able to befriend others for she was a natural friend to any in need. Such people are essential in a church setting. The lonely or the bereaved may simply need a friend on whom they can call when things get tough; this will probably be for a set period until they come to a place of security or wholeness.

- Then there will be the **pharmacists** – a group of people who will be excellent at doing general type praying. If you have an earache or a headache, you will probably visit the pharmacist for his help before you trouble the doctor. These are the kind of people on your team who are able to listen to the person whilst listening to the Holy Spirit at the same time. They then dispense His help quite quickly and effectively. Pharmacists will probably be used as ministry team after or during the Communion Service, during healing services, during house groups or as part of pastoral teamwork. This is a very useful way to accustom people to ask for prayer in a non-threatening setting. Inviting the Holy Spirit to come, listening to Him and ministering using the gifts of the Holy Spirit as He gives them. Some people are very gifted in this type of ministry for they hear God, and can pray quickly and to the point!

- Thirdly, there is the **doctor level**. These are the people on the Pastoral Prayer Ministry Team who will be experienced at praying for people in greater depth. Prayer at this level takes much more time and may be provided in a number of ways. For example after the evening service when people are not as rushed or those who are 'doctors' could be available in the church office or vestry on a certain day through the week, for deeper levels of prayer. Alternatively, ministry may take place through an appointment system. The 'doctors' on the team will minister into deeper areas of need such as sexual abuse, human spirit wounding, deliverance or relationship needs.

  Prayer ministry at 'doctor' level will usually take much longer than 'pharmacy' praying, maybe between one and six sessions, depending on the person's story and his or her need. It is important to stress again that such praying should not be done alone for the reasons given above.

- The **consultant level** is where the person seeking help needs the support of someone with a much wider and deeper knowledge in a particular area than the 'doctor' is able to give. Usually ministry will be offered into more specialist areas such as freemasonry, New Age religions, the occult, bereavement or marriage counselling.

I am encouraged to hear of all that you are doing Avril, let me know how you progress during the next few weeks. You certainly seem to be taking great strides forward.

Love in Jesus

Ruth

Letter 11

Praying for Others

Dear Avril,

You have asked me a number of times what your prayer ministry team needs to know when they are praying at 'pharmacy', 'doctor' or 'consultant level'. At last, I have found a few minutes to write and advise you what areas they will need to be familiar with in order to pray in an effective manner. I will begin with the 'pharmacy level' and I am going to make a list for you Avril because it will probably be much easier as a quick reference.

'Pharmacy level'

- They need to learn how to listen to the person in need and to the Holy Spirit at the same time. Please assure your team this does become easier with practice!

- They need to know how to move under the anointing of the Holy Spirit. They need to be able to discern when the Holy Spirit is moving amongst the people.

- They need to learn how to move in the gifts of the Holy Spirit and be willing to submit to His directions.

- They need to learn how to be sensitive to the person's undisclosed needs, for they will probably share some areas of pain but not others.

- They need to understand the importance of forgiveness: a vital key to healing.

- They need to know about the importance of godly and ungodly bondings and how to break the person free from the ungodly ones.

- They need to realise when they are out of their depth and whom to contact in order to pass the person on for deeper level prayer.

'Doctor level'

- When this happens the person will need 'doctor level' prayer and the 'doctors' on your team will need to know all of the above plus:

- How to listen to the person's story and take relevant notes.

- How to break ungodly bondings as well as how to lift off any demonic influence that may be there.

- They will need to know how to discern the roots of pain and trauma, whether they spring from the emotions, the spirit or from the physical area.

- They will need to know how to pray into different situations in some depth. If they are ministering to someone whose situation is beyond their knowledge then they will need to arrange to pass the person on to the 'consultants' on your team.

'Consultant level'

- At 'consultant level' your team will need to be trained in all of the above plus:

- A knowledge of varied and deeper subjects such as: bereavement counselling, the depths of sexual abuse, freemasonry and the importance of demonic strongholds. You will hopefully also have people on your team who know how to pray for children, women's problems, the occult, marriage counselling and the influence of the New Age. Not every 'consultant' will be knowledgeable in each of these areas, but they will probably 'specialise' in two or three fields of knowledge. They may come to you and say that they are out of their depth, for example if they suddenly find themselves dealing with satanic ritual abuse or deep brokenness of spirit. The person will then need to be referred to a 'hospital', for example Ellel Ministries or some other place that deals with the specific area of need.

I hope this helps you Avril.

Love in Jesus

Ruth

Letter 12

'Pharmacy Praying'

Dear Avril,

In answer to your query regarding how to pray into various situations with which you may be confronted in church, I am happy to give you some general ideas for praying at 'pharmacy level', although even here we need always to be open to the Holy Spirit changing the schedule! If you are training members of your team to be 'doctor's' or 'consultants' then of course a different format of training will be necessary.

How to pray for inner healing at 'pharmacy level'

- Remember that you cannot delve as deeply into a person's life, as you would if you were dealing at the 'doctor level'.

- Remember that the presenting symptoms may be physical but have an emotional root.

- Ask the person some relevant questions: 'When did the problem begin?' 'Did anything happen around that time?'

- Explain to the person what you think may be happening in their life.

- With their permission, begin to pray into the emotional area of the memory they have just shared with you.

- The person will probably have built up barriers around the pain. Try to ascertain how they usually deal with their pain.

- These protection mechanisms will need to be repented of, and permission given to the Lord to dismantle them.

- Ask the Holy Spirit to bring the memory, and the pain associated with the memory, to the surface.

- Wait on the Holy Spirit for any words of knowledge, discernment or wisdom as to how to pray into the memory and the pain.

- Pray into specific areas of pain. For example if praying into 'shame', keep lifting it off the person. Persevere with one emotion until you feel it has been dealt with. Don't jump around from one emotion to another.

- They may need to forgive anyone who has caused or added to their pain.

- You may need to break any ungodly bondings between the people involved.

- As you pray the negative emotions out, pray the positive emotions in. For example:

  Lord Jesus I ask you to lift all shame off Jane, shame for her part in the failure of the marriage. We ask you to remove any false sense of shame. Father we ask you to speak to Jane of your acceptance of her. Give to her a sense of your delight in her, etc.

- When you feel that the emotional pain/memory has been dealt with, pray in the peace of the Lord Jesus Christ. Speak the Word of God into the person as the Holy Spirit brings it into your mind. You may need to pray for any physical ailments at this point also.

- Be willing to follow any directions, which the Holy Spirit may give you, as to how to proceed.

How to pray for the abused at 'pharmacy level' (verbal, physical, emotional or sexual)

- Be very sensitive to the person's feelings, because it takes a lot of courage to seek for help. Be especially careful not to be shocked or judgmental.

- Be aware that the person will probably only share the **'tip of the iceberg'** as they come forward for prayer.

- Be especially careful not to touch the person without asking them for their permission, e.g. laying hands on them to pray.

- Believe their story, however unusual it might be.

- If there were very deep issues, we would suggest that you have a general prayer and then suggest that they have a personal ministry session later.

- If the issues are not so deep then proceed as follows: lead the person in a prayer of repentance for any part, which they have played in the abuse. Speak forgiveness to them in Jesus' name.

- Establish the lordship of Jesus over their lives.

- Lead the person in a prayer of forgiveness towards the person who has abused them.

- Look for all the ungodly bondings, which have been established because of the abuse and break them in the name of Jesus. It is especially important to break the bond, which will have been established with the first person that abused them.

- Note the emotional pain and begin to pray as suggested in the previous inner healing prayers.

- Break the power of any pronouncements which the abuser may have spoken over them, or inner vows the person themselves made as a consequence of the abuse.

- Prayer may be needed for any physical damage, which the person may have suffered.

- Note the possible emotional areas where deliverance may be necessary, for example fear, shame, guilt, etc.

- If it seems right, be prepared to pray firmly but gently into the demonic. Lift off the spirit of the abuser and any other spirits, which you discern, are present.

- Be willing to be led by the Holy Spirit as to further ministry.

How to pray for deliverance at 'pharmacy level'

I would caution you, Avril to teach your team members never to assume or go looking for a deliverance ministry! They certainly need to be on their guard and look out for any indications of the demonic but never to assume it. The following are some of the ways in which they may read the signs.

- As you listen to the **person's story**, you may begin to discern the enemy's footprints.

- The person's **behaviour** will also give you some clues. For example: hands pointing, eyes rolling, back arching.

- It may be that you find that you develop a sense of **discernment around the demonic**. I still remember quite vividly the day when I was in a certain person's presence and suddenly felt that I could be physically sick. It was only later that I discovered that she was a practising witch! If you think the demonic is present, you need to make the following decisions:

  (a) How **deep** does it go?

  (b) How **experienced** am I in the area of deliverance?

  (c) How **confident** am I of my authority?

- Agree with your co-partner whether to pray into this area or whether to arrange a personal prayer session for the person in need with the Prayer Ministry co-ordinator.

- If you agree to pray, these are the following steps, which you should follow when praying at 'pharmacy level':

  - Pray **protection** for the person, their family, yourself and your family.

  - Get the person to pray a prayer of **repentance** for his/her sin and **renounce** the enemy.

  - **Bind** the enemy and speak out your authority in Jesus over him.

  - Keep **alert** to what the **Lord** is doing and keep listening to the Holy Spirit.

  - Keep alert to what the **person** is doing.

  - Keep alert to what the **enemy** is doing.

  - Watch for any **manifestations**. The enemy will often reveal the place where he is hiding. (For example once when I was praying with a girl from Malaysia, she suddenly clutched her stomach. She had been into Buddhism and had been dedicated to the **Goddess of Mercy**.) Don't worry if there aren't any obvious manifestations; just press in if you are convinced that demons are present.

  - **Address** the enemy firmly, without shouting, basing your authority on the Word of God and insist that he depart from the person.

  - Keep **pressing in** until the person feels and knows a release or you feel in your spirit that the enemy has gone and the Holy Spirit has concluded what He wishes to do on this occasion.

  - Remember that you don't have to do everything, just what the Holy Spirit tells you to do.

- Pray that the Holy Spirit will **fill** the vacated area with Himself, and seal the door so that the enemy cannot come back with his friends!
- Suggest to the person that they need to fill their **minds** with the Word of God.
- Ask the Holy Spirit for a passage for them to study.
- Suggest also that they need to meet frequently for **fellowship** and **prayer** with others in the Body of Christ.
- If you feel that there is more work to be done, suggest to the Prayer Ministry co-ordinator that a **follow-up session** may be necessary.

How to pray for physical healing at 'pharmacy level'

- Ask the person relevant questions regarding the illness/ infirmity. For example: 'How long have you had it?' 'When exactly did it start?' 'Can you remember if anything else happened at the time?'

- Keep alert to the fact that there may be emotional or demonic roots.

- Raise faith in the person and yourself by speaking out the Word of God. For example, Jesus said we were to lay hands on the sick and they will recover. Agree with the person that that is the desire of the Lord and the desire of our hearts.

- Begin to pray into the physical pain. Release all distress. Release all fear associated with the illness. Release all pain and fear of pain.

- Speak healing into the particular area of need.

- Speak the creative healing power of the Holy Spirit as He guides you.

- Ask the person if anything is happening. You are looking to see what God is doing.

- Keep praying and pressing in as long as it seems right.

- Keep open to the Holy Spirit and His gifts, e.g. words of knowledge.

I do hope that this helps you Avril, as it is only a rough guideline. As you know every situation is different and each person is unique. I am looking forward to hearing from you soon.

Love in Jesus

Ruth

Letter 13

Using a
Pastoral Prayer Ministry Team

Dear Avril,

I am conscious that I am giving you all of this advice which may seem rather overwhelming at first but I hope that you will appreciate that it takes time and patience, as well as hard work, to implement all of the above. In the meantime, it is important to give the Lord the time and the space to heal and touch people in the regular worship meetings of the church; in other words letting folks '**learn by doing**'.

We have already mentioned some of the methods used, when healing is to be a continual part of the life of the church. The following are some other ideas which you may incorporate:

- After a Sunday service, you could have people available to pray with others either at the front or in a more private setting. It is better if you try to make it a regular and an expected part of the time spent together.

- Maybe you could have a prayer board onto which people could pin 'prayer requests' and a time in the service when there will be prayer for those in need.

- A regular time in the service when people can quietly speak out the names of those needing prayer.

- A time provided at the Communion table for people to have hands laid on them and prayer made. This can be a very effective means of praying, especially in the more traditional churches, where people are not used to moving freely around the church in response to expressed needs. Sometimes simply having the bread and the wine available in a quiet corner for individuals to partake of privately, if they so desire, can also be a very helpful means of healing.

The Pastoral Team could pray in people's homes, at the owner's request, praying into whatever needs have arisen. Maybe you could hold a healing service for the churches in the area, every three to four months. This could either be on a Sunday evening or during the week depending on the needs and the programme of the church and the neighbourhood.

Eventually you will probably find that there will be a requirement, within the congregation, for more in-depth ministry and this can be achieved in a number of different ways:

- Leadership may recognise a need in a person or in a relationship and with the person's agreement, format a six to eight week programme of prayer ministry, discipleship and study with selected members of the Pastoral Prayer Ministry Team. This will usually be with those who feel called to the 'doctor level'.

- You may decide to have the church open one afternoon a week, e.g. Tuesday 2–4 p.m., and have a rota of team members available, who are willing and able to be there on a regular basis. You could circulate the local churches, with the availability of prayer, coffee, and chat.

- If you train the ministry team in specialised areas, e.g. bereavement, marriage guidance, abuse, etc., then they could be available to members of the congregation, or other churches, if and when necessary. You will probably find that when they are trained the needs will present themselves.

- Another possibility is to have a telephone service, either locally or on an area basis for people to ring in to request prayer and/or help. A number of people committed to praying for such requests can be a dynamic way of bringing healing and building faith.

- Have prayer requests at your local clinics and doctors surgeries (with their permission) so that people can pop a prayer request into a box, either for private prayer or with a request for a personal ministry session with members of the ministry team. The requests could be totally anonymous if desired and a member of the ministry team would collect these each week.

- A coffee shop (drop-in centre) in the middle of town where people can receive care, comfort and a chat, or to arrange appointments for a personal ministry session.

As you can see Avril, there are multitudes of ways in which Pastoral Prayer Ministry Team people can be used to good effect. There is no 'one way' – only the right way for your fellowship, and I'm praying much that you and leadership will find it.

Love in Jesus

Ruth

Letter 14

Working Within the Anointing

Dear Avril,

I am so glad that you are beginning to feel that a Pastoral Prayer Ministry Team is now coming together in your fellowship and that you can see how the Lord seems to be opening up opportunities for them to be used. Thank you also for sharing with me which **particular** area of your church life you feel that the Lord primarily blesses. I was so encouraged that worship is such an important element amongst you folks. I would strongly advocate you to work within that particular anointing. Some churches have an anointing for 'evangelism'; some for 'worship' and some for 'teaching' and the Pastoral Prayer Ministry Team needs to flow with and work alongside the church's main calling. It is still true today, as it was for Jesus that

> 'The Spirit of the LORD is upon Me,
>   Because He has anointed Me to preach the gospel
>   to the poor.
>   He has sent Me to heal the brokenhearted.'   (Luke 4:18)

True healing will only flow when Jesus, through the Holy Spirit, is present to heal and it is important to ask the questions: 'Where is the anointing? What area of our church life does the Lord particularly bless?' All or most churches are involved with the 'full gospel' but usually they will have a different emphasis. The following are some of the questions Avril, which you will need to ask both of yourself and eventually the leadership of your church.

- What is the heart of our church?

- What is our overall vision?

- Where is the anointing?

- What area of our church life is God blessing?

- What is our church's main calling?

- What is its **prime** purpose?

- Is it a **worship centre** where God's glory is displayed? For example 'The Church on the Way' led by Jack Hayford is such a church. The main focus is to lead people into worship, which eventually brings forth in them a need and a desire for healing as they draw near to the heart of the Father.

- Is the main thrust of the church to make new Christians? Is it a **conversion unit**, to evangelise the area? Is its job to convert people, equip them and send them out onto the streets to make more Christians as soon as possible? If so, then the Pastoral Prayer Ministry Team will be mainly used alongside the evangelists to help set people free from some of the areas of bondage and pain which they will undoubtedly have brought with them into the Kingdom. Evangelism inevitably calls forth a need for healing.

- Is it a **teaching school** to build up the saints, where the main purpose is to provide deep theological teaching? Is its main purpose to nurture and disciple Christians of long standing so that they come to a place of holiness? If so then such teaching will inevitably raise areas of need that the Pastoral Prayer Ministry Team will need to address. We used to call this a 'process of sanctification'!

- Is the church of which you are a member a **hospital**, whose main calling is to minister to the wounded? A place where all of the needy and the desperate seem drawn. Is it continually providing care for the broken? Nursing them back to health if necessary, maybe over a long period of time? If so then you will become known as a place where other churches may send their long-term sick and your Pastoral Prayer Ministry Team will be kept very busy!

Depending on the vision and the heart of your church your ministry team will therefore be used in different ways: for example as an evangelistic tool to help clean up folk after they have become Christians; as a means to train and make disciples; as a resource for leading people towards holiness or as a way of responding to worship. It is so important to work with leadership and to discern with them as to where they see the main emphasis of the church and work within that.

Love in Jesus

Ruth

Letter 15

Problems You May Encounter

Dear Avril,

I wouldn't want you to assume that establishing a Pastoral Prayer Ministry Team is totally **'problem free'** (as if you would!) and therefore l feel it is only fair to warn you in advance of some of the difficulties which you may encounter. For example, one of the main problem areas in local church is that people may be very diffident about opening up to people whom they know well and who thought that they knew them!

- This raises the issue of trust and confidence. Very often people feel safer sharing with a stranger, so building trust is something that you will have to work on, and this takes time and patience.

- Church schedules can also be a bit of a problem. If there is something on every evening or people are so busy with other things, you and the potential team members will have to decide on priorities. It can be so easy to put everything else in front of training, learning and praying together.

- Another area of potential difficulty is that of standing against accusations (spoken or inferred) of superiority. For example, a church may decide that the Pastoral Prayer Ministry Team will use badges on a Sunday in order that any visitors will know whom to approach for prayer. Unfortunately, this could give rise, within the team and the congregation, to a feeling of either 'We are better than you' or 'Who do you think you are'!

- You will need to watch your Pastoral Prayer Ministry Team for signs of burnout. People who have a heart for others are usually very self-sacrificing and give out so much that there is a tendency for them to either burn up or dry up!

- When dealing with, and praying into other people's lives, you open yourself up to possible spiritual pollution. The enemy may try to get some of the pain or the dirt from the other person to stick on to you. If this happens you will need to know how to pray cleansing for one another, after prayer ministry times. It also helps if you are aware of 'why' and 'how' we are polluted through prayer ministry sessions if only to be forewarned. For example:

  - There may be an area of **weakness** in us, which has not yet been dealt with and the enemy can move in on it.

  - Maybe we have a very **sensitive** human spirit, which notices the other person's pain all too readily. We need to learn how to protect our spirit and yet still be open and available to the other person.

  - Of course if we are living in areas of **known sin** this will give the enemy a foothold and we shouldn't be surprised if he hits us. To begin to minister in a state of known sin is really asking for trouble.

  - Entering ministry when **very tired** is also not recommended as this can lead to mistakes in ministry, as well as opening yourself up to the possibility of becoming spiritually polluted. You will find, if tired, that you begin to operate in your own strength and not out of a place of rest This may lead you to begin to pray in an attitude of sympathy and not with empathy thus causing you to become drained physically, emotionally and spiritually.

– Another danger is getting into prayer ministry times **unprepared**, and this can happen for a number of reasons – e.g. lack of time or personal preparation. However, we have found that if the Lord takes us into a ministry situation unexpectedly then He assuredly will undertake for us.

– There is always the danger of '**dustbin raking**', in other words listening to unhealthy details simply for the sake of it. If you put your head into the dustbin, the enemy may leave a **smell** on you!

– Sometimes the enemy will bring an **unprovoked attack** through the person you are ministering to, and the means of pollution will then be varied depending on the situation. It may be the use of words and pronouncements. For example: 'You are a pathetic minister' 'How did they ever let you join?' 'You're no good and never will be.' Alternatively, in the worst possible scenario, it may even be a physical attack, hence the advantage of ministering in twos.

– It may be that the **demonic** will hit your body with tiredness, weariness, or heaviness during the ministry session.

– Sometimes the **soul area** may be hit, bringing confusion of mind, a mixture of emotions, or wrong emotional tie with the person you're praying with causing transference of pain etc. It is important to recognise that feelings can transfer during a ministry session. You may suddenly be confronted with feelings of anger, depression or guilt. A sense of uncleanness, heaviness or tiredness may descend on you during or after ministry.

– It is important to know how to deal with pollution when it comes. The vital thing to remember is that you need to be aware of the possibility, and be mindful of the need for personal preparedness.

– Remember to pray protection for yourself, your family, and the person you're praying for, and learn to know the power of the Cross as your protection.

– Learn to develop strength in your human spirit. If you speak in tongues use the gift regularly. Learn to protect your spirit as well, e.g. using the shield of faith to quench any fiery darts or the breastplate of righteousness to guard your heart.

– Know the safety of working in a team, for unity is essential; stand together without judging one another. Aim to develop a team where it is safe to confess needs, weaknesses and sin and where it is possible to request prayer if anyone feels polluted. The following are some of the ways we would deal with pollution:

(a) **Recognise it**. In other words admit it is there. Ask questions of yourself: 'What is happening here?' Did I feel like this before?' Recognise Satan's attack and resist it. Establish the root, where did it spring from? 'Is it because of weakness, tiredness, or is my spirit too vulnerable?'

(b) **Pray for yourself**. Use praise and worship, for this will take you into God's presence, and use the Word of God, for it is a means of cleansing. Also plead the blood of Jesus over yourself (1 John 1:7–9).

(c) **Confess** it to one another as recommended by James (5:16) remembering to be specific and requesting that others pray for you.

Having shared some of the problems with you Avril, which will undoubtedly arise as you continue with your team, I would encourage you to stay with it for there are certainly more rewards than obstacles. I urge you therefore to hold onto your vision until it is accomplished.

Love in Jesus

Ruth

Letter 16

Resource Material

Dear Avril,

Of course I am very happy to send you a sheet of sample prayers, which you can photocopy and use for your Pastoral Prayer Ministry Team. You will probably find that most of them are already incorporated in the Basic Training Course material, but I quite agree that it is sometimes helpful to have them on one sheet. The ministry team will probably need to lead the people through these prayers phrase by phrase because, in my experience, the folk who are being prayed for are often a little nervous when in a ministry situation!

A prayer of repentance

Heavenly Father I thank you for the forgiveness, which you offer me, through the death of Jesus Christ upon the Cross. I agree with your verdict on my sin, that the punishment is death. Thank you that Jesus died in my place. I freely and gladly confess my sin [*ask the person to speak out anything specific*] and I turn away from it in the name of Jesus. I choose to turn from my sinful ways and go your way from this day and I thank you, in Jesus' name. Amen.

A prayer of forgiveness

Ask the person to speak out the names of the people they are choosing to forgive.

> Heavenly Father, I thank you that Jesus died upon the Cross to take away my sins. Thank you that you have forgiven me. I now choose, by an act of my will, to stand with your command to forgive those who have hurt me. I therefore freely forgive [*name of the person*] for all of the harm and the hurt which he/she has caused me. I freely release him/her into the freedom of my forgiveness. I ask you to release me now from all of the consequences of the hurt and pain in Jesus' name. Amen.

A prayer inviting Jesus to be Lord of each area of the person's life

> Thank you Jesus for dying on the Cross to set me free from my sin. I now choose to declare that you are Lord of every area of my life. Lord of my home and my family. Lord of my time and my possessions. Lord of my work and my finances. Lord of my thoughts and my emotions. Lord of my decisions and my future. I give myself, spirit, soul and body to you. Thank you for being my Lord. Amen.

A prayer confessing the sins of the family line and breaking any ungodly links

> Father I thank you that on the Cross you have dealt with my sin through the death and resurrection of the Lord Jesus Christ. I thank you too, that according to your word, I can come and confess the sins of my ancestors. I do gladly and humbly repent of the sins, which my family line have committed. I especially repent of [*ask the person to speak out any specific sins which they know the family have committed*] and also any false worship which they have been involved in [*ask them to speak out any that*

are relevant, e.g. freemasonry, spiritualism, Buddhism, etc.].
I ask you to forgive the sin and that you will set myself
and my family free from its consequences, in Jesus name.
Amen.

A prayer to set people free from any curse of words or pronouncements

Father, I thank you that on the Cross Jesus carried my
curse. I stand now in His name against any words or
curses, which have been spoken against my family line
or me. I believe that Satan and all of his works are under
the feet of Jesus and I reject such words and curses and
declare myself free in Jesus' name. Amen.

A prayer to set people free from any ungodly bondings

In the name of Jesus Christ of Nazareth, I break every
ungodly spirit, soul or body bonding between [*name*]
and [*name*]. I take the sword of the Spirit, which is the
Word of God, and I declare that [*name*] is set free from
any hold, either natural or demonic which [*name*] has
had over her/him. I place the Cross of Jesus Christ
between [*name*] and [*name*] and declare that all ungodliness be drawn to the Cross. I command, in Jesus' name
that all demonic activity which has taken advantage of
the ungodly bonding to hold [*name*] in bondage, to go
from [*name*] and never to return. Amen.

After completing all of the prayers, invite the Lord Jesus to fill
the person afresh with His Holy Spirit.

I have listed some areas of the occult and false religions
which many folk have been into and I am sending it to you
with this letter. We find it particularly useful during ministry, as folk tend to forget what they have been involved in,
unless they have it listed in front of them. Anyway use it if
you feel it would be helpful; otherwise please feel free to pass
it on to someone else who might be able to make use of it.

Most common false religions

Buddhism, Christadelphians, Christian Science, Confucianism, Freemasonry, Hare Krishna, Hinduism, Islam, Jehovah's witness, Moonies, Mormons, New Age, Scientology, Shamanism, Spiritualism and Transcendental Meditation.

Occult involvement

Acupuncture, amulets (horseshoe mascots), Ankh (a cross with a ring top), astral travel, astrology, automatic writing, black magic, chain letters, charms or charming (for wart removal), Chinese astrology, clairvoyance, colour therapy, contact with a corpse, coven involvement, crystal gazing, divining, Dungeons and Dragons, eastern meditation, fortune-telling, Gothic rock music, gypsy curses, handwriting analysis, hard rock music, heavy metal music, hex signs, homeopathy, horoscopes, hypnosis, incantations, iridology, levitation, martial arts, mascots, mediums, mental telepathy, mind control, mind reading, necromancy, occult literature, omens, ouija board, pagan fetishes, pagan rites, palmistry, pendulum diagnosis, phrenology, psychic healing, satanism, séances, self-hypnosis, star signs, superstitions, table tipping, talisman (divining by charms), tarot cards, tea-leaf reading, temples of other religions, thought transference, transcendental meditation, witchcraft and yoga.

Quite a list isn't it and I am sure that there are many more!

Reference books

Whilst I am sending you these resources I decided to include some of the books, which we would be encouraging any ministry team with which we were involved, to eventually read. Some may be out of print but it would be worthwhile to try to borrow them from friends or buy them second-hand.

▶ **The practice of counselling**

The Search for Significance, McGee, Word UK.
In Search of Self, V. Axline, Penguin Books.

Handbook of Counselling, Stephen Palmer and Gladeana
McMahon, Open University Publications.

▶ Marriage

Women – God's Secret Weapon, Ed. Silvoso, Gospel Light.

Men Are from Mars, Women Are from Venus, John Gray,
HarperCollins.

The Five Love Languages, Gary Chapman, Northfield
Publishing/STL UK.

▶ Bereavement

A Death in the Family, Jean Richardson, Lion Publishing.

A Grief Observed, C.S. Lewis, HarperCollins.

Dragonflies and Maybugs (a little booklet to use with
bereaved children).

On Death and Dying, Elisabeth Kubler-Ross.

▶ Deliverance

Healing Through Deliverance (Part 1 & 2), Peter Horrobin,
Sovereign World Ltd.

Deliverance and Inner Healing, John & Mark Sandford,
Victory House.

Demons Defeated, Bill Subritzky, Sovereign World Ltd.

Christian Set Yourself Free, Graham Powell, Sovereign World
Ltd.

▶ Emotional healing

Healing Women's Emotions, Paula Sandford, Victory House.

Deep Wounds, Deep Healing, Charles H. Kraft, Servant
Publications.

Healing for damaged Emotions, D. Seamands, Alpha
Publishing.

Healing Emotional Wounds, Ruth Hawkey, New Wine Press.

Emotionally Free, Rita Bennett, Kingsway Publications.

The Transformation of the Inner Man, John & Paula Sandford, Victory House.

▶ **Healing for children**

Dear Mark & Sarah, Beryl Burgess, New Wine Press.

Praying for Children, Ruth Hawkey, New Wine Press.

▶ **Human spirit healing**

Healing the Human Spirit, Ruth Hawkey, New Wine Press.

Comfort for the Wounded Spirit, Frank & Ida Mae Hammond, Impact Books.

▶ **Generational sin**

Freedom from Generational Sin, Ruth Hawkey, New Wine Press.

▶ **Mental health**

Why Do I Feel So Down When My Faith Should Lift Me Up?, Grant Mullen M.D., Sovereign World.

Caring Enough to Forgive, Augsburger, Gospel Light.

Caring Enough to Confront, Augsberger, Gospel Light.

▶ **Abuse**

Healing Victims of Sexual Abuse, John & Paula Sandford, Victory House USA.

Unlocking the Secret World, Wayne & Diane Tesch, Tyndale IVP.

Tapes, videos and courses

There are so many tapes and videos available from a number of different churches and Christian Healing Centres and so I hesitate to name individual ones. It is probably best to scour your local book shop and friend's tape decks to see what they have been listening to and ask them what they would recommend. Having said that, the video *Frozen Peas* is an exceptional video about sexual abuse and some of the Ellel Ministries' tapes and videos from their conferences and courses are excellent and can be very useful indeed.

We do hope that these resources help you Avril. Please keep in touch and let us know how you are doing, as we are looking forward to visiting with you soon and meeting up with your team to share some ideas.

Love in Jesus

Ruth